To Leslie
Who keeps me young!
(at Pilates!)
Love
Linda
x

71/100 Lph.

Linda Lines

MEN IN MY KITCHEN

POETRY · LOVE · RECIPES

_____

Photo & Graphic Credits

All photos by Linda Lines except:
- Old black & white family photos.
- Page 87: Photo borrowed from Motcomb Street party website.
  motcombstreetparty.co.uk
- Page 117: Courtesy of Savoy Hotel London.
  http://Fairmont.com/Savoy.
- Images of Linda - by Roger Eaton roger@rogereaton.com

Logo: A collaboration between Oscar Lines and
Hagar@littlegreenmonkey.co.uk

Graphics: Little Green Monkey Limited.

 About Linda

My life has been a series of re-inventions – I was raised in the West Country, but my father's and first husband's RAF postings gave me an appetite for travel, and I have spent the rest of my life in cities; I did poorly at exams, but later read psychology and set up a nursery school in Singapore which is still going 40 years later.

On returning to live in London with my young son in 1975, I was injured when Scott's Restaurant in Mayfair was bombed by the IRA. After my recovery, we went skiing in Austria, where I met a group of financial advisors from London. This led to my training in the City and founding The Lines Partnership, a small financial management company which prospered until I sold out, leaving me, three husbands later, free to pursue the four passions which inspire me: writing poetry, photography, cooking and travel, all happily combined in *Men In My Kitchen*.

Ever since I retired from the City, I've tried to stretch the summer for as many months as possible – I write better when it's warm and sunny. I love to work, relax and play in the sun. Writing poetry seems more important to me than anything else now. The poems are not just any poems – they are my true stories.

In this, my first published book, there is a story in each poem and they go from the present day on a brief journey back to both my mother's and my grandmother's 1950s kitchens and then slowly forward again to the present. The verses are full of small but haunting truths, transforming my own experiences into what I believe to be universal.

This growing collection has many sources, many kitchens I have known and loved that have shaped me and provided the backdrop to pivotal moments in my life, which I would like to share with family, friends, all the men who have dared to venture into my kitchens and with you.

I hope you enjoy the linked recipes too. They are an important part of the story. Some are extraordinarily easy and encourage short cuts and all are treats that delight in adding a little something extra.

The *Men In My Kitchen* **iBook** is available, where I recite all the poems, should you be tempted to listen rather than read. The writer's interpretation can change the way you may think about each poem. There is also an introductory video and a collection of my own photographs, offering an additional dimension and making the **iBook** a more visual experience. The **Kindle** edition has no frills: the poems, recipes and the same linked photographs for non-Apple users.

My new website, lindalines.co.uk, launched at the same time as *Men In My Kitchen* and broadens the spectrum. This is where I add projects as I write them and it already includes a short story, more poems and a gallery of photography, with much more in the pipeline. This is just the beginning... I am already hatching the next series...

Table of Contents
Poems and Recipes

My Kitchen
Knows Me Well

My kitchen knows me well… I would live in it
Bathe in its welcoming warmth. It's always there.
The heady smells and tastes… from golden to brown…
The touch the textures, the magic words
"Leave to improve for forty minutes"
From chaos to calm, clean and tidy in less
It is always there…

Put a man in my kitchen, and magic…
I am at my best, my very best.
The anticipation, the preparation,
The candles, the wine… all combine to make my heart sing
The music divine, we laugh, we sing… we dine,
We love… we laugh, we cry… we sigh…
Ahhh…
My kitchen knows me well.

RECIPE: BREAD RECIPE……WITH A TWIST

There is nothing like home-made bread – made easy – and no shame in ready-to-use bread mixes. They can be wonderful – and oh so quick! All you usually need to do is add water and vegetable oil. Only choose mixes that are top quality and UK-based with local ingredients. Choices include sourdough, whole meal, spelt – and there are organic breads too. Follow the instructions carefully and then make it yours by adding some excitement of your own.

Here are a few of my favourite additional ingredients that have transformed and delighted, from my garden – by the handful:

- Fresh rosemary, chopped or bruised and softened with mortar and pestle
- Sage and onion, chopped
- Any chopped, mixed, fresh herbs: parsley, sage, thyme, marjoram, etc.
- Walnuts
- Olives
- Strong cheese, grated or diced
- Sun-dried tomatoes
- Sea salt and black pepper, liberally added
- Seeds such as sunflower or caraway

My most important tip:

To help the bread mix rise, leave it for a good 40 minutes to improve in a warm place. Watch it double in size and then bake it!

You can put the dough in a bread tin to rise, or make it into whatever shape you like: round like a cottage loaf or long and oval…

Be adventurous with flavours and shapes.

I Dream
In My Kitchen

I dream in my kitchen... of those men in my kitchen
The first hellos... and the fond goodbyes...
And everything in-between
Hearts mended and broken... words not spoken
Light music, right music, wrong music
Dance music – oh I have danced!
Between courses (hors d'oeuvres and dessert)
I have dined... I really don't mind...
Spicy hot salsa... romantically entwined
The food combines with all the senses
To lift and lighten and brighten...
There are many stories to tell...
Wait awhile...
And I'll make you smile as well!

RECIPE: SPICY HOT TOMATO SALSA

Meanwhile, why don't you get comfortable with my Spicy Hot Salsa recipe, which only takes 10-15 minutes to prepare, grab a glass of something cool, and escape with me right now! Go on, indulge yourself!

Ingredients:

- 4 plum tomatoes, chopped
- 1 clove of garlic, crushed
- Half a cup of red onions, finely chopped
- 2 small hot red chilli peppers, finely chopped (de-seed for less spicy… add more if you dare!)
- Juice of one lime or half a lemon
- Season with sea salt and freshly ground pepper

Method:

Combine all the ingredients in a glass bowl.

Chill until ready to serve.

Garnish with a fresh herb (parsley / coriander / basil).

Serve with tortilla chips or Melba toast.

The leftovers are good in pasta the next day, served with a green salad.

I Cook In My Kitchen

My kitchen, where I stand and cook –
Come with me let's take a look.
Black marble tops on which to work
Are polished to a sheen
With baby oil, a trick I've learned
from helping hands that clean

It's order that makes my pulses race,
of all the things I use
I've grown to love these tools of joy,
Each item in its place…
Poised to help me through my art
Of making taste buds sing
Most preparation is by hand, of gadgets not a trace
Instinct and senses are the thing… so not a lot of bling.

I save that for the table top… mine is made of glass
It floats above the polished tiles, it's in a different class…
When laid and set with candles lit, it sparkles in the night
And lifts me to another place where stars won't take a fright
To meet a rival from down there… that glitters as they do…
My own appearance matters too…
A mood of peace and calm pervades when everything is done
The scene is set, the wine is chilled, my heart skips a beat
He pulls my chair out as I say… "Let's eat."

RECIPE: WARM ORIENTAL SALMON ON A BED OF GREEN SALAD LEAVES

This is a light, romantic meal, which you can serve with warm sourdough bread or new potatoes garnished with butter and chopped chives to make more substantial. Keep it simple... there are other things to think of! Delicious served with your favourite chilled rosé wine...

Ingredients:

- 2 fresh fillets of salmon
- 2 egg cups of medium dry sherry
- 1 egg cup of light soy sauce
- 1-2 spring onions, chopped
- 2 large portions of mixed salad leaves

Method:

Set the oven to 180°C / 350°F / Gas 4.

Place the two salmon fillets in an ovenproof dish lined with enough tinfoil to cover and seal.

Pour over the sherry and soy sauce.

Sprinkle with chopped spring onions.

Now seal and bake in the preheated oven for 15-20 minutes. Check after 15 minutes whether the salmon is pale pink throughout.

Add more of the same proportions of sherry to soy sauce if it isn't happily swimming in the juices. Don't let it dry out – you need the juice!

Divide the salad between two dinner plates, then lift out each salmon fillet carefully and place them on top of salad.

Spoon over all the juices evenly. The juice acts like a warm salad dressing and should be plentiful.

I Dance In My Kitchen

I remember Fahad... A Syrian War Lord he said
Oh he could dance... endlessly
We did... in my kitchen.
Bar Cuba was the place we met... Salsa was the thing
Warlords and Cuban music loud
No need of dance floor or a crowd
A complete CD from beginning to end,
And how we danced in my kitchen that night
To heaven I was sent... It was clearly meant.

He loved slow-cooked lamb, I like to please.
Simmering for hours, marinated well...
In rosemary and garlic... Ahhhhh... what a smell
The Latin music combined with wine
As he whisked me round the floor,
And we were breathless we two
Oh I remember Fahad...
My kitchen loved him too...

RECIPE: SLOW-COOKED SHOULDER OF LAMB IN GARLIC AND ROSEMARY

Lamb is such a rich, juicy meat, so full of flavour, that when cooked slowly to my recipe, it falls off the bone and is perfect served very simply with a crisp green salad garnished with chopped mint and a little olive oil and lemon juice. Season to taste and serve with a strong rustic bread to mop up the juices. A red, robust full-bodied wine is a must.

Ingredients:

- 2kg Welsh shoulder of lamb – properly hung that's as good as it gets
- A big bunch of fresh rosemary
- 1 whole head of garlic
- Olive oil
- A small glass of red wine
- Salt and freshly ground black pepper

Method:

Score the fat side of the lamb all over with a sharp knife.

Lay half the sprigs of rosemary and half the garlic cloves on the bottom of a high-sided roasting tray.

Rub the lamb all over with olive oil and season it with salt and pepper. Place it in the deep roasting tray on top of the rosemary and garlic and arrange the rest of the rosemary and garlic on the top of the lamb. Make small slits with a sharp knife and push it in. Pour over the glass of red wine, season again with salt and pepper, then leave it to marinate for at least four hours or, preferably, overnight.

Tightly cover the tray with tinfoil.

Preheat your oven to 200°C / 400°F / Gas 6 and place the tray in the middle. Turn the oven down immediately to 170°C / 325°F / Gas 3 and cook for four hours – it's done when you can pull the meat apart easily with two forks.

The Conservatory

There are men in my kitchen today,
to give me more space to play
The thought came and went, all savings would be spent,
But it came back to haunt me again
A conservatory adds potential… so yes, it's essential
I rationalised… so don't be surprised…
The voice in my ear went on
All that noise, dirt and pain could drive you insane
If there were not compensations of sorts…
Strong men with good legs… in shorts.

Men's humour abounds, it's tea all round
Had my heart soaring at the thought…
Hmm, so much to be bought
Those strong muscles on show, this idea could grow…
Would add to my bountiful life.
All that planning and drawing,
Points here to be scoring,
Better than the one next door
Now my heart's soaring,
At the thought of more flooring
In this wonderful visionary space.
Expand new horizons, create something surprising
Throw caution out of the way
There are men in my kitchen today.

RECIPE: WARM POLISH APPLE CAKE

This cake is best eaten warm with either ice cream or delicious warm custard and is reasonably quick to put together. Please note the batter will be thick, which makes it one of those cakes that need to be eaten the same day.

Ingredients:

- 1 cup of self-raising flour
- 2 tablespoons of sugar
- 1 egg, lightly beaten
- 3 tablespoons melted butter
- 3 tablespoons milk
- 2 soft desert apples, peeled, cored and cubed
- 1 teaspoon cinnamon and 2 tablespoons of brown sugar for sprinkling on top

Method:

Preheat the oven to 180°C / 350°F / Gas 4.

Grease cake tin or pie dish.

Sift the flour and add the first portion of sugar and then the egg, melted butter and milk and mix well.

Pour the mixture into the greased tin/pie plate.

Mix the cinnamon and sugar together.

Arrange the sliced apples on top and sprinkle with the sugar and cinnamon.

Bake in the oven for 30 minutes or until a skewer comes out clean.

Serve it to workmen for elevenses or afternoon tea... or both if you want to be popular. Good with tea or coffee.

My Grandmother's Kitchen

No men in my Grandmother's kitchen...
Unless you sat Grandad down to eat,
The moment that you heard his feet
Come down the garden path,
His train driver's work complete.

Yet one more thing to do for him
before he cycled home.
Each day this faithful task
Of railway sleeper cuttings
Discarded from the past.
He'd take them home for firewood
Where nothing burned so well
Creosoted as they were, only he could tell.

Bike in shed and wood went too
Just one more thing to do
Rid that smell of soot and coal
And belching red hot steam
Difficult it's true, this was his goal.
Oil cloth hat on hook and hands well scrubbed,
He'd barely time to listen...
All smells combined in that kitchen...

Her scolds and loving hands were deft, no need to guess
Each meal was set in stone
Leftovers from Sundays stretched to Mondays
Of which bubble and squeak came first
Fried egg on top crisply cooked, if not how he'd frown
His greenhouse tomatoes, cut fresh down,
Oh the smell of them…
He grew his own… they were his pride
No word yet been said, till butter on bread
and a cup of strong tea by his side.

This moment was his… no children allowed,
We were all playing outside…
In silence he ate till he'd cleaned his plate,
Which promptly went into the sink
With a sigh and a burp
He loosened his shirt… and
Moved to his favourite chair.
As he lit up his pipe and happily sighed…
My Nan's expression was coy…
With that deep grumpy growl of a man that's content,
He looked Nan full in the face…
"Oooh cariad" he said… his endearment for her since a boy.

Men in my Grandmother's kitchen? Oh no, we knew our place…
The routine not quite over yet, another stage to go
She turned her back and, pinny off, waved to us 'come in'
Well-rehearsed and in the know,
Playing by the Coop
Until that signal came, we stayed away from him
Our treat for such collusion was our fizzy pop
Our Nan had glasses all in line and filled them to the brim.
We gathered round, our faces shone
And then we ventured in
At Grandad's feet, we spread around
We grinned at what came next
He shooed us off with twinkling eyes
Then magicked out his tin
Of Mintoes tightly wrapped in green,
They were his favourite thing.
He teased and played, we couldn't reach
And then our Nan came in…
Fair play, we'd caught one each she said
And now we had to go… upstairs to bed
She chased us up and read
Her happiness complete
No one left in my Grandmother's kitchen now…
And Grandad's fast asleep…

GRANDAD'S RECIPE: BUBBLE AND SQUEAK

Now this is the epitome of comfort food. Quick and easy too... The crisp slightly over-browning is as it should be... ask my Grandad!

Ingredients:

- 1 tablespoon of fat from roasted duck, meat or chicken
- 4 rashers of streaky bacon, roughly chopped
- 1 red onion, chopped
- 1 clove of garlic, crushed (optional)
- Leftover Brussels sprouts, boiled cabbage, cold mashed or crushed boiled potatoes (leftover roast potatoes can also be used)
- 1 fried egg to put on top

Method:

Melt the fat in a large non-stick pan, allow it to get nice and hot, then add the bits of bacon. As they begin to brown add the onion and garlic, then the sliced sprouts or cabbage and let them colour slightly for about 5-6 minutes.

Add the potatoes and stir everything together in the pan, turning frequently.

Allow the mixture to catch slightly around the edges. It's the bits of potato that catch in the pan that define the term Bubble and Squeak.

Don't worry, let the mixture brown. Turn it out onto grand-dad's dinner plate, make a small well in the top and add the fried egg, quickly cooked in the same pan leaving it soft in the centre and crisp around the edges.

A cup of strong tea and two slices of buttered bread would be expected...

My Kitchen In France

I have a kitchen in France, that I shall share with you…
Dans la belle centre ville, I happened to see,
Down a tiny cobblestone rue,
A gatekeeper's house that's medieval
In the grounds of the ancient Collégiale.
Once stood proud and tall, and part of the wall
It stood there looking at me
"Won't you come inside to see?"

With it's jettying timber frame
Above what once was a door, such a shame.
No floors, inside walls or stairs,
With pigeons nesting in pairs…
I could see straight through to the sky.
I felt my heart sigh as I wondered why,
It had been left in this state so long…
Two months later I bought for a song.

There are many hidden secrets in France
All hoping for that second chance.
Whilst economies tumble and Euro is humbled
Be tempted to take a look… See my house now
With all the work done, a place in the sun
Twelve months of hard work, it's a gem,
Working with a lot of lovely French men
Who put their heart and soul in this
To them I owe more than a kiss.

The kitchen is the house's heart
I decided from the start.
We wouldn't compromise at all
Authentic walls and stairs and floors
And really old oak doors were lovingly restored
With latches found in antiquaires where too long they'd been stored.
With help from friendly artisans
Who'd helped with all the plans,
We scoured the country north and south
Some help from word of mouth.
We put our heads together then
At first, with three strong men.
With materials from days gone past,
We knew that they would last.

From local poplar trees and and oak, interiors built on site–
It had to be just right
The local maçon built the stairs, suspended them in space
From right inside my kitchen with extraordinary grace.
Now every time I visit there, front door thrown open wide
My eyes just stand and stare... they fill with tears of disbelief
To think that it is mine... this house now, so fine.

The moment that I go inside and see the work we've done,
The house looks back at me once more
And knows just what's been won.
It's honour, love and empathy rolled up into one
Artisan's skills with charm and wit, whose praises will be sung
For many years to come...
In that corner of Southwest France,
Won't you come inside and glance?

I love to share this treasured space with those that really care
They're usually good friends I love that like to hide away
There's something special in the air that forces you to be
A better person than you were, especially for me
It's cooking in my kitchen there...
That's my favourite place to be...

RECIPE: MAGRET DE CANARD ET LA SAUCE ORANGE ET ARMAGNAC

Pan-fried Duck Breast with Orange and Armagnac Sauce

In Southwest France, every part of the duck is cooked and eaten. It is tasty, affordable and popular. As was the Frenchman who taught me this recipe... as delicious as the rich red local wine he selected... mmmmm.

Ingredients:

2 large duck breasts with skin (200 grams each)

For marinade:
1 tablespoon each of honey, balsamic vinegar, Armagnac
Zest of 1 orange
Mix all ingredients together.

For Sauce:
2 tablespoons course cut best quality marmalade
Juice of half a large lemon
1 measure of Armagnac.
Slowly bring to boil all ingredients and simmer for 2\3 minutes, then set aside.
Serve warm on the side with duck breasts when cooked.

Preparation:

Score skin of duck breasts diagonally and place in a deep dish.

Pour prepared marinade over the duck breasts.

Refrigerate for 2/3 hours.

Method:

Remove from fridge to return to room temperature.

Take a heavy frying pan, non-stick is easier.

Remove duck from marinade and drip dry on rack over marinade bowl.

(5 mins). Cook breasts fat side down first, over high heat for about 5 mins.

This creates smoke so have extractor fan on full!

Remove breasts on to a clean plate and turn heat down to medium.

Pour excess fat into cup. Return breasts to frying pan, flesh side down, for a further 5 mins, making sure just enough fat to cook with. Remove duck breasts back to plate, then add back some of the duck fat for last stage.

Turn heat up high again, and when hot, return breasts, flesh side down to pan for 2/3 mins whilst basting skin with spoon. The red hot fat basted over the skin will produce the final crispy, golden brown skin.

Remove to plate and allow to rest for a good 5 mins before serving sliced or whole. The duck will be pink, but not bloody, and very very tender.

Serve with warmed Armagnac and marmalade sauce, after adding and simmering any marinade left in bowl.

These duck breasts are popular when served with large sauté potatoes and a crisp green salad... and a rich red, full bodied wine... of course.

The Break-Up

There's a man in my kitchen and I'm far away
In Thailand for winter where the sun shines all day.
A great place to work, rest and play,
My brother's eldest has come to stay.

He sent me an email, a sad tale of woe,
He'd ended his relationship, so where could he go?
Sleeping on sofas in friends' flats had made him feel low,
So somewhere quite peaceful to get his head straight
With a decent kitchen to soothe his sad state.

So that's where he is as I sit here and write,
To do it just fills me with honest delight.
I imagine him pottering in the warmth and the smells
Of something he's cooking, how my heart swells.
Only time will tell,
So much love in that kitchen, he'll feel it I know…
All sad experiences help us to grow.
There's a man in my kitchen
I'm happy to know…

RECIPE: NEPHEW PAUL'S TEXAN SLOW COOKED CHILLI

Warming and comforting, long, slow, soothing… simmering away for hours…

Ingredients:

- 2kg of beef chuck or brisket cut into small chunks
- 2 large dried Ancho chilies
- 2 large dried Poblado chilies
- 2 fresh chilies, the type depending on how spicy you want it
- 2 red onions
- 12 cloves of garlic
- 3 red, yellow, green or mixed bell peppers

- 4 tins of chopped tomatoes
- 400ml coffee
- 2 cinnamon sticks
- 3 teaspoons of smoked paprika
- 3 teaspoons of cumin
- 2 teaspoons of dried oregano
- 2 bay leaves
- 3 tablespoons of molasses
- Olive oil

Serves 8

Method:

Soak the chillies in the coffee for 5 minutes.

Fry the chopped onion, paprika, cumin, oregano and bay leaves in olive oil in a large pan or casserole dish for 15 minutes over a medium heat.

Slice and deseed the chilies and add to the pan along with the chopped garlic.

Then add the tomatoes, coffee and molasses and season with salt and pepper.

Add the chunks of beef.

Simmer over a very low heat for at least 4 hours – the longer the better!

Remove the chunks of beef and shred them using two forks.

Add the chopped bell peppers and fresh chilies and cook for a further 30 minutes.

A Poet In My Kitchen

There's a poet in my kitchen, same age as my son.
He's tall, dark and handsome and his life's been hard won.
Of my life now he's a very big part
And inspired me to make a new start
He's stolen many a heart…

In spite of what he's overcome
His story of abandonment left me undone.
From Ethiopia he came when hardship struck,
With his mother who loved him, such sadness and pluck
The ultimate sacrifice she had to make
Short-term fostering for his own sake
But the authorities made a terrible mistake
He was given for adoption and sent far away
To Scotland - where he thought he was Scottish
For ten years and more
Until they too, showed him the door.

Sent to a turmoil of change you could not conceive
The stories of heartache you wouldn't believe
To hide what he knew was happening to him
He toughened resolve to escape what was grim, and wrapped himself in
To a fantasy world and let nothing in
By nature kind and good and so anxious to please
No one cared or listened for so many years
He was let down.
How he came out I never will know
And turned into the wondrous man I now know

He's risen above all of that pain
And shakes off shackles and never complains
A lesser man would have been driven insane.
He's risen to stardom with his wonderful sound bites
By expressing such beauty in all that he writes
He gives night and day with all that bruised heart
I'm proud I helped to play just a part
When asked to find him a place he could hide
To write what he's good at and have peace by his side
So pleased to be able to give him that chance
A month by himself in my house in France.
Oh how he loved it, and France loved him,
Now he's a regular visitor dear
And changed my life too, that's clear
In an extraordinary way, it's true to say
There are two poets now in my kitchen today.

RECIPE: DORO WAT - ETHIOPIAN CHICKEN STEW

Doro Wat is an Ethiopian spicy chicken stew –which is slowly simmered in a blend of mouth warming spices. Easy, comforting, delicious, and so easy to make! African comfort food at its best. This version of Doro Wat is authentic and easy to put together. It is packed with robust flavours from the spices you will find in ready-made Berbere spice mix, and spiced butter adding great dimension to the dish and an incredible depth of flavour. Easy to buy both spice mix and butter on line, or Ethiopian market.

Ingredients:

- 2 ½ - 3kg whole chicken cut in pieces, or selection of pieces preferred.
- 3 tablespoons spiced butter (can substitute with vegetable oil) or ¼ cup canola oil
- 2-3 medium onions sliced
- 1 tablespoon minced garlic
- ½ tablespoon minced ginger
- ½ tablespoon paprika
- 1 tablespoon tomato paste
- 4-6 large soft boiled egg, shelled removed
- 2 tablespoons Berbere spice
- 1 tablespoon dried basil (optional)
- 1-2 fresh lemon
- 2-3 cups of water
- salt and pepper to taste

Serves 5-6

Method:

Season chicken pieces with salt, pepper and set aside.

In a large heavy pan, over medium heat, add spiced butter and onions.

Sauté onions, stirring frequently, until they are deep brown - about 7-10 minutes.

After the onions are caramelised and have reached a deep golden brown, add more oil, followed by the Berbere spice, garlic, and ginger.

Stir for about 2-3 minutes, for the flavours to develop and the mixture to turn a deep rich brown colour. Be careful not to let it burn.

Then add the 2-3 cups water.

Add chicken, tomato paste, basil, salt and cook for about 30 minutes.

Add the whole eggs; gently mix to ensure that the eggs are immersed in the sauce.

Continue cooking until chicken is really tender about 10-15 minutes or more.

Adjust sauce thickness and seasoning with water or broth, salt according to preference.

Serve warm.

Traditionally Doro Wot is served with a flat Ethiopian bread.

Brown steamed rice is also good.

No Men In My Kitchen Today

No Men in my kitchen today,
because it is Valentine's Day
I'm decidedly not cooking ....no way!
... I'm in Thailand far far away
Where the chill of winter has NO say

The tropical heat makes me unwind
All cares aches and pains left behind
There is no place so kind to me
There's no better winter place to be
Than sitting in the sun...
My heart it has won,
senses are completely overcome

Lotus-eating hedonistic place said one
A massage and food paradise oh come!
Which is why, Sunday brunch at Barai,
And you may well ask where?
Is this place without a care…
A Thai wooden house above the beach
With a verandah of foods beyond belief
So elegantly prepared a variety of stalls
From sushi to oysters, and little fish balls
Lobsters and all fruits of the sea
Couldn't improve upon for me.
A delicate breeze means no pain,
As the Thai girls and boys pour the champagne.
The barbecue offers more
of delicate marinated meats galore
And a Philippine duet harmonises their score.
No more needed to say?
No men in my kitchen today.

Picture Gallery
Enjoy the gallery of images from that day in Hua Hin
at the Regency Hyatt's executive hideaway, The Barai

My Mother's Kitchen

My mother's kitchen when I was young
Must have been where all this began.
Which is odd, because way back then
In her kitchen, no sign of men.
Just my big sister, little brothers and me
Life felt so free...

The Second World War had come and gone,
Leaving hardship of which I knew none.
I remember rationing and thought it the norm
To learn to do without,
To work hard in the kitchen, there was no choice.
Even now I hear my mother's voice.

Using herbs from the garden,
And things we had grown
From seeds in winter we all had sown
…Our own.
Early rhubarb, salads and beans,
The tomatoes and potatoes, the best you'd seen.

Everything valued and lovingly stored
In jars for the winter… we'd never starve!
Nothing was wasted, everything kept
For that moment when needed… mum never slept.

A little imagination went a long way,
Is something often my mother would say.
How to make something taste really good
With no eggs, butter and sugar if you could.
They were indeed a scarcity,
And luxury food a rarity…
But she just somehow did.
Steamed puddings and dumplings in stew,
These things she really knew how to do.

She taught me to knit and to make do and mend
As there was so little left to spend.
Shoes and clothes all well worn,
Neatly mended when torn.
The hardest thing for me to bear
Were my sister's hand me downs, not fair!

So few men around to observe,
So when they came back, a big learning curve.
For women had risen well to their task,
A lot of independence at last...
My mother was my role model then,
It never came from men.
When Dad came back a stranger to me,
He was only in the kitchen for tea.
That's what we called it then,
Oh, and his name was Ken.
The RAF was his life,
Not at home with us and his wife.
The world was suddenly full of change.
Peopled with lots of men, life became strange!
Not knowing what to do then.

It never affected me... or so I thought,
Until now...
These memories have bought
An insight to me.
When I look back now and see,
How all that I am and all that I feel
Came from those times oh so real,
But in truth now seem surreal.
It really explains a lot to me of who I really am
And why I stay in my kitchen so much,
And cook as well as I can.
Why I care as much as my mother did
As if I'm waiting like her,
For answers so I'd be rid
Of that anxiety I sensed in her.
Waiting for that man to come,
The one that's in your dreams
And then he never measures up,
That is how it seems...
You wanted so much to be surprised.

Needed something quite profound,
Or say they knew just how hard it was
To stay at home... housebound.
A father and mother all rolled into one
Is what she was to us, and found it suited well.
Something good at which she could excel.

Dad simply couldn't be, the man she'd hoped to see.
Wrapped up in his own sad times and missing out so much,
A father and master of his house, how could he be?
Things weren't the same you see.
He tried hard to adjust to this person in his place,
But guilt came in and filled that space.

He recognised she'd earned her right.
These unsung heroes that remained out of sight.
How could he explain...
This feeling of loss and tell her of his pain?
I often wondered why she cried,
But I always knew Dad tried.

She taught us the things we needed to know,
That would last us all of our lives...
We know well now how to survive,
But never said thank you before she died.
It never occurred to me 'til now, how much she really did.
It helps to understand all too well, what happened later on,
When She left our Dad for another man,
Who put us all through hell,
And said he understood her better.
My anger dissipated after reading her last letter.

So many women in her shoes, who were simply not the same
After the War they fought in too, but on a different plain.
No they are not to blame.
And the men changed too, and sacrificed their place in home and
hearth.
My heart goes out to them the most, they'd missed the biggest
part.
Of watching children growing up, it just breaks my heart.
As we needed guidance from them too, I'm sure that's true.
It left Dad impotent and sad with nothing left to do,
No chance of being close to us, it simply was too late.
He went about his business then, and closed the garden gate.

Growing up with a Dad elsewhere and him alone out there,
I'm waiting for my man to come home,
And show him how it was…
To discover those joys I had when young,
The ones that they did not.
It's because they missed so much back then
That I want them all to see, how much love
In my kitchen these days…
And why I have time for them.

RECIPE: SPOTTED DICK

The name of this pudding always made my brothers laugh...

Ingredients:

- 240g self-raising flour
- 240g currants and raisins, soaked in brandy
- A pinch of salt
- 150 ml cold water
- 120g shredded suet
- 90g sugar
- A teaspoon of sugar to decorate

Method:

Sieve together the flour and salt, then add the shredded suet, sugar and dried fruit and mix with enough water to make a firm dough.

For the traditional shape, roll into a large sausage 20cm long and roll up in a pudding cloth.

Place in a pan of boiling water, cover securely and boil for 2 hours.

Turn the pudding out onto a hot dish, sprinkle with the sugar and serve with custard.

Suggestion:

If you want to make a Spotted Dick in a basin, grease a 1.1 litre pudding basin and steam for 2 hours. Turn out and serve as above.

My Son's In My Kitchen Today

My son's in my kitchen today.
He stops in the park on his way,
To run and let off steam,
While I cook and dream
About chasing his cares away.
He's usually too busy to stay
On a weekday…
So these precious moments I treasure,
And concentrate on culinary pleasures.
Simple ones that make him smile,
As only he can do,
As long as it's not chicken stew…
And we don't dwell on the past,
When food was made to last.

At all costs I avoid chicken stew.
The memory haunts me still.
I really made him ill.
The chicken roasted on day one,
Next day was served sliced cold.
Day three not so old for including in a bun,
For my one and only son.
Day four you have to boil the bones,
And set the meat aside, for adding later on.
Then slice and peel all veggies you can find.
Add salt and black pepper you can grind.
Fresh mixed herbs or dried from a pot,
They really help a lot.
But never, never after that,
Try to stretch it more.
Never heat it up again,
Even if you're poor.
We've travelled far and wide since then,
And developed quite a taste
For all the finer things in life.
Not leftovers cooked in haste.

His childhood favourite, and mine too,
Is macaroni cheese.
Sliced tomatoes grilled on top,
Cheese golden brown to please.
This simple pleasure served with wine,
That's red and rich and fine.
No point in cutting corners here,
I'd never think of beer.
"Really nice to see you, mum"
That smile again…
"Glad you could come, my darling…
Cheers!

RECIPE: MACARONI CHEESE

An old family favourite... With many tips passed down from parents, grandparents... and now multiple on-line choices. I believe the success lies in making the cheese sauce. Master that and you can add excitement in a number of ways.

Ingredients:

- 700ml full-fat milk
- 1 onion peeled and cut in half
- 1 garlic clove
- 1 bay leaf
- 350g macaroni
- 50g butter
- 50g plain flour
- 175g-250g of grated mature Cheddar cheese.
- 50g of grated Parmesan or any leftover blue cheese can add extra bite
- 1 tsp English mustard (or 2 or horseradish also adds bite)
- 50g grated Parmesan
- 50g coarse breadcrumbs

Method:

Prepare the macaroni

In a small pan, warm the milk, add onion, garlic and bay leaf until almost boiling.

Remove from the heat, leave covered to absorb flavours for 10 mins, then strain.

Cook the macaroni 3-4 mins less than pack instructions until nearly soft, but still with a little firmness (in Italy, known as al dente). This will take about 8-10 mins. Drain in a colander, then rinse under the tap and stir to stop the macaroni sticking together.

Next - the roux!

Whilst a roux is simply flour added carefully to melted butter and gently cooked, it is essential you don't rush this process. The key is cooking it long enough. Too little and it tastes raw. Too much and it tastes burnt.

Melt the butter in a medium saucepan. When foaming, add the flour, then cook, stirring constantly, NOT LESS than for 1 min on a low heat.

To finish the sauce, slowly stir the warm infused milk into the roux until smooth. Simmer for 3-4 mins, stirring often, until the sauce has thickened and coats a wooden spoon. My mother would run her finger through the sauce on a spoon – it should leave a trail!

Remove the pan from the heat, then add two-thirds of the grated Cheddar cheese and mustard or horseradish.

Season, then stir until all the cheese has melted.

Heat oven to 190°C / fan 170°C / gas 5 and grease an ovenproof dish with butter (I use a 25 x 18cm).

Assemble and bake

Pour the cheese sauce through the macaroni to coat it well, then tip into the prepared dish. Sprinkle the Parmesan, remaining Cheddar and breadcrumbs over the top. A family favourite is to decorate with sliced tomatoes.

Bake for 15-20 mins until golden brown and bubbling. Serve piping hot on its own or with a green salad. For hungry young men, a jacket potato with crispy skin, compounds the felony.

There's A Liar In My Kitchen

He lied and he lied
...and I cried
He didn't know I knew the truth
...from quite early on
In a state of disbelief the charade carried on
Until I could face what I had learned
From someone close who told
She knew his tricks of old.

This man I'd met in Motcomb Street
I liked him straight away
We had plenty to say
I liked his story too
of working in the City
Just the same as me!
And both of us were free

I was invited out next night
And liked him even more
His manners a real delight
Such happiness in sight
Dinner, movies and romance
He even liked to dance!

So many things in common
Which doesn't happen often.
The weeks went by...
He told me why
He and his wife had parted
And the legal process started
I believed with all my heart
When he said this was our new start...

You see he had a wife who lived in France
She trusted him to work away and visit at weekends
She even bought his tickets well in advance.
He'd cheated on her many times before.
If I was her I'd have shown him the door
He'd promised her when she first found out
To reform... and got a second chance...
No, I was not the only woman he'd entranced.

He had a father old and frail he used to hide the trail –
Behaviour in my book beyond the pale –
And said that's where he was those times
He couldn't visit me
Oh why I didn't see?
How could he pretend that way?
Should I make him pay?
But how to find a way
That won't punish others too?
What would you do?

I hugged the hurt so close to me
And prayed that she was wrong
Confronting him with all I knew
Was begging for reprieve
I feared he'd turn my head again
So well practised to deceive.

Instead I tightly laced my thoughts
How to tackle this pain he'd bought
The worse for all the intimacy
That had seemed so right to me.

It culminated in my kitchen when
My heart screamed out no more!
It was time to even out the score
As I mustered up the courage
And hardly dared to breathe
To say I didn't care for him
So would he kindly leave

I cared for someone else I said
Who was coming back to stay
Honesty and simplicity meant everything to me
Not causing pain and duplicity
That's the nearest that I came
At hinting I'd uncovered his game.
My heart bled, when all was said
He simply hung his head.

I could not bring myself
To tell either of them the truth
To share my anguish and pain
Where is the gain…?
So until this day, he's home free
Which doesn't feel quite right to me
I'd love to find a clever way,
Something really quite cool,
To show him that I found him out and I am no fool.

How to put a wrong to right
To give him such a fright
He'd never try again
To inflict such pain
Destroy that trust
Yes I simply must…
Without hurting others too
Tell me, what would you do?
I've decided now… let honesty prevail
Tell it as it really is, write it down like this
How he lied, and he lied
…and I cried…

RECIPE: DEVILS ON HORSEBACK

Dismissing 'Sour Grapes' and Deadly Nightshade
Feeling like a Gooseberry Fool,
Quickly dropping Bombed Alaska,
Sweet outside... a cold secret within
I settle for Devils On Horseback
They transform from sweet ripe plums
To dried wrinkled prunes in disguise
Wrapped in tasty streaky bacon
Such a surprise, they'll out those lies!

Ingredients:

- Agen dried prunes are the best ("Pruneaux d'Agen")
- Smoked streaky bacon is tastier.

Method:

Remove the stones, or buy pitted prunes.

Pre-heat the oven to 190°C / Gas 5. Cut each rasher of bacon in half.

Wrap each half around a prune, secure with a wooden skewer and place onto a baking tray.

Bake for approx 30 minutes or until the bacon is cooked and golden.

Turn over after 15 minutes.

Place onto a decorative serving tray and serve.

A Secret In My Kitchen

There's a man in my kitchen
Who freely comes and goes
To take care of clever things,
That I cannot
He's been here from the start
And yes, he still plays a big part.

As our separate lives expand and grow
He'll be here, we both know.
His love and loyalty still show
No need for more.
He gives stability
I'm there for him and he for me
Still friends, and how it ought to be…
Not something we talk about:
My happiest secret, no need to shout
Yet I feel he's always there
Some things I'll never share
Or tell you who he is
And that I still care.

This man gave his all to me
And taught me what love is
Nothing was too much for him
There's nothing he wouldn't do
He gave and gave and didn't care
What others close might think
He said so once without a blink.

His heart was open wide
Such love that came from deep inside
It overwhelmed me
With the responsibility
What happened to maturity?

I simply let it go… for that moment
For such a short time
We soared to untouched heights
His youth and innocence sublime
But not a crime
For me to love him so.

I knew it couldn't last
But whilst it did
I gave back and forgot the past
And he gave more…
Made my heart soar.
I tried to make him strong
For when this would be 'our past'
Such intensity could not last
I knew it from the start.

So gave the best we could
And bared our very souls
And soared to heights unheard.
Perhaps it sounds absurd
Oh how we cared
That summer down in France
When we led the world a dance
To protect those close to us now
To keep our secret.

He insisted not, he was proud
He'd shout his love out loud
The secret would be out
It only needed one
He told.
It sewed the seeds of doubt
The magic was undone

A year flew past and winter came –
I always get away –
Of course he had to stay….
With tears in our eyes
A few heartbreaking sighs
We knew the time had come
No words needed, just pain –
How could things stay the same?

That Spring when I came home
He was waiting there for me
The way he stood had changed
I could not complain
With difficulty we refrained
From close embrace
His crumpled face, so strained
I could clearly see how things would be
He was not the boy I used to see…
My months away had set him free
He'd risen to the challenge.

He's grown and now a better man
Than most, we are still close
The best a friend could be
And still always there for me …

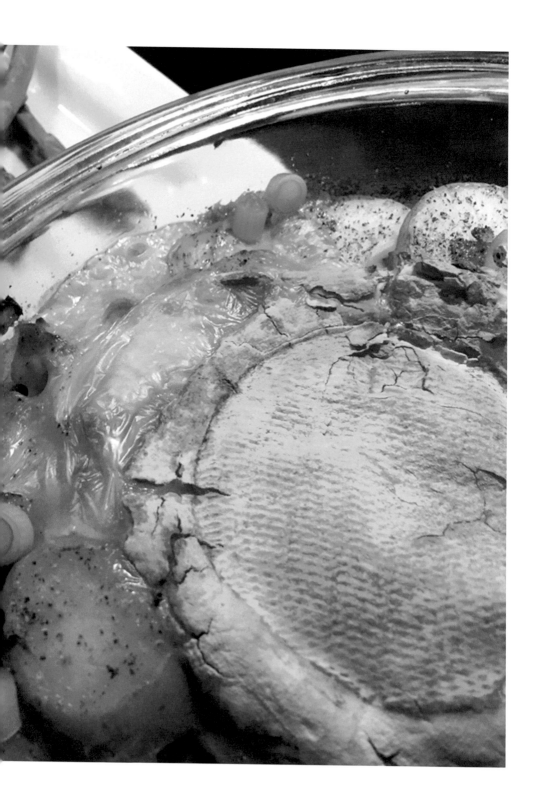

RECIPE: TARTIFLETTE

Tartiflette comes from the Savoy region of the French Alps. It is made with potatoes, Reblochon cheese, lardons and onions – very comforting and filling.

Ingredients:

- 1.2kg firm potatoes
- 2 large onion, sliced
- 200g lardons or 6 rashers of smoked back bacon, diced
- A whole 250g Reblochon cheese
- 40ml crème fraîche
- A large glass of dry white wine (optional)
- Vegetable oil
- Salt and black pepper.

Method:

Set the oven to 180°C

Prepare in a gratin dish.

Peel the potatoes and cover them with cold water in a saucepan. Bring to the boil, check with the tip of a knife to see they are tender, then drain and allow to cool.

Sweat the onion in a frying pan with a little oil. Do not brown.

Add the diced bacon and cook for a few more minutes.

Cut the cooled potatoes into thick slices and arrange half of them in a layer in the gratin dish.

Add half the bacon and onions.

Season each layer to taste.

Add layers of the remaining potatoes, bacon and onions.

A glass of white wine may be poured over the top.

Spread the crème fraîche on top.

Cut the Reblochon in half and place it on top of the potatoes.

Put the dish in a hot oven and bake it for 15 minutes, or more if you like it really golden.

A glass of white wine poured over is optional.

Serve with a green salad or wilted spinach … And the remainder of the dry white wine.

Or even a French claret...

Talk About Men In My Kitchen

Over a cup of strong tea
Earl Grey for me
Or maybe coffee and cake...
On a white bone china plate?
Oh for heaven's sake...

Tell the truth before I throttle...
Susie, just open the bottle!
Let's go up to the roof
Where, when all's said and done
Our best stories come
and way more fun, so
Let's take some eats
And a few more treats
Everything else is there.

Let's loosen up and tell the truth
No secrets up there on my roof!
Dispel that frown
Come sit down
What's happened to put you down?

Up there in the late afternoon sun,
Summer just begun
My roof garden a hideaway
The perfect place to have your say
Summer fruit ripening, shirts undone
It's where the best talking's done
Begone drudgery.

Tell me all
"Oh what skullduggery!"
Let me top up your glass.
What more could you ask
From a well equipped bar
And wine cooler too?
The perfect place to bask
To sip fine wine
To talk and have fun
Up here the truth will out
In the late afternoon sun...

CRUDITÉS WITH A TWIST

When a friend has a need... and comes to call... no time to plan!
Whatever happens to be in your fridge that day, or cupboard, be inventive, be creative. Speedy presentation and colour is everything!

Cut and slice almost any vegetable/salad ingredient into slender sticks. Sugar snap peas and radishes add vivid colour and are perfect as they are.

Dips can be made from canned or chopped fresh tomatoes, chickpeas, etc. Just blend and add a little spice, chilli sauce, olive oil and seasoning to taste. Add fresh herbs to garnish or chop and add to your dip.

Raw veg, nuts, tortilla, crisps, canned veg, olives are usually to be found hiding in my cupboards. Lumpfish caviar is having a revival, so a tiny jar is useful in the fridge. On top of halved quails eggs is particularly tasty.

Another favourite: Endives make a natural scoop for cheesy dips, or split in half with creamy blue cheese crumbled on top.

Then open the bottle... and off you go.

Cocktails In The Cotswolds

A great honour it's true:
Asked to concoct something new
For the very privileged few
At a famous exotic event…
Where cost can make a dent
Unless you're corporately sent.

The brief was a summer cocktail
For a new aphrodisiacal brew
In a Cotswold kitchen I knew…
An enthusiastic team assembled then
We stood around the kitchen sink
The best place in which to think…
Predictably "Blue Dream" for the men
For ladies of course it had to be pink
Ingredients came easy, nothing too sleazy?
With pomegranate, grenadine and plum brandy
Champagne on top would be dandy
To soften the shocking pink shade
Or else we might not get paid.

Knickerdropper Glory came with ease…
Totally designed to please…
We tasted our way through a lot
They truly were really small shots…
Of liqueurs and ingredients
Discarded if not expedient
Measurements not exactly lenient
My I feel hot…

To taste first, 'Blue Dream' for the men
Could I lend my tastebuds again?
As long as it won't make me poorly
Peach brandy and Curaçao… surely?
Two parts lemonade mixed
With plenty of ice is the trick
Garnish with blueberries
And white chocolate chips
Shaken not stirred, and nothing absurd
Then take just a little sip
Now I feel sick…

And so to Sussex…

To the scene of the event let me take you
To a countryside's midsummer dream
In West Sussex it would seem…
Where people dress up, it's tradition
Whatever the weather's condition
In elegant evening wear
Haughty men stare
At the ladies with shoulders bare
Who dare…
Pink and Blue cocktails abound
In those wonderful stately grounds
With picnics set up all around
On immaculate lawns… to operatic sounds
Candelabra and tents, exotic scents
Of flowers and expensive perfume
No worries of economic gloom
The performance starts soon…
A race to empty the glass
Gulped down now there's class…
More champagne? No, I pass…
… Out…

COCKTAILS

Concocted in Prue Leith's kitchen.

KNICKERDROPPER GLORY

For boys to give to girls (makes 2–3 cocktails)

Ingredients:

- Large teacupful of liquidised watermelon
- Same amount of pomegranate juice
- Two tbs coconut cream from a can or box
- Two large measures of Grenadine or white plum brandy

Method:

Mix together the fruit juices and the coconut cream.

Pour into a shallow container and freeze.

Put cocktail glasses into fridge or freezer too.

Just before serving, chop the frozen mixture into chunks and liquidise to gravelly/sandy texture. Spoon into the glasses. Pour a good measure of grenadine or plum brandy, or two, over each. Garnish following red fruit on a stick: raspberry, watermelon, fig and a mint sprig.

BLUE DREAMER

For girls to give to boys (makes 2–3 cocktails)

Ingredients:

- Chill blue Curaçao
- Barak Palinka (Hungarian Apricot or Peach Brandy)
- Lemonade (or tonic water for a more grown-up taste).
- Chill the glasses too

Method:

Mix one part Curaçao, one part brandy and two parts lemonade or mixer in a shaker or jug with ice and pour into the glasses. Garnish with fresh blueberries and white chocolate chips.

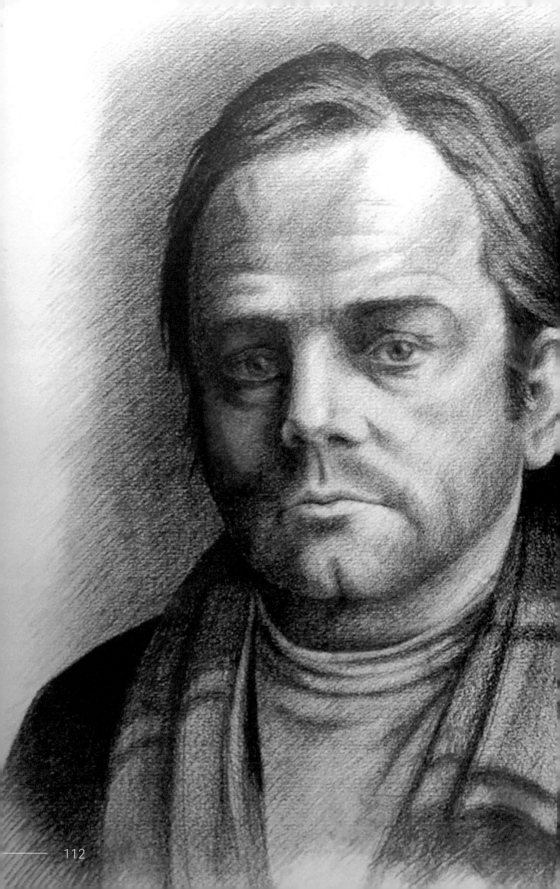

Artist
In My Kitchen

A tribute to Lincoln Taber (1941-1989)

He had presence
He had passion –
Not a follower of fashion –
He had style
He had wit
In all he said and did,
The stories he told
Adventurous and bold
This man just glowed…

Always a smile on his lips –
To watch him paint
Was a privilege…
With magic in his finger tips
With a delicate touch,
Never too much,
He mimicked real life
To deceive the eye…
Which is the truth
And which is the lie?

Each day a special event
A journey of surprises
Fleetingly lent…
I sat for him and listened
He looked intent, absorbed,
Enthralled, and captured
The essence of me
On canvas… for all to see.

He loved life with wide-open arms
And was loved back in spades.
Such was the case at The Savoy
On the completion of his trompe l'oeil
Such realistic imagery
Never lacking in charm
Or cheek…
One day he took me to peek
At the view from the roof
Of this famous hotel
He knew so well.

"Like a Canaletto painting"
He said... I nearly fainting
As through the kitchen we went
Collecting delights offered en route
Bubbly and glasses
Followed suit
"Chef won't tell" –
Like a naughty schoolboy
With no loud ringing bell
Telling us to stop –
A picnic to end all picnics!
What a treat, up there on top
Of the world...

Known there well as he was
And definitely because
He was...
Loved...
And now so missed.
His legacy not quite enough...
But leaves us crying after love.
Still my heart sings:
Memories are everything
A talent lost too soon
And never forgotten...

My Grandson In My Kitchen

In a blink he is full grown
How did that happen, I groan,
Those long arms and legs all over the place
He curls up like a spring
Then grins… at me
With ease and such grace.
All smiles and innocence
On that beautiful young face –
Yesterday a babe in arms
Today a young man
Whom I want to protect from harm.
He wants a motorbike… what!
Driving lessons I knew about –
What does your father say?
… I shout.
He doesn't know… yet
He'll blow his top, I bet.
Silence… pain, fear…
Helpless… what next?

I cook his favourite meal
By special request, that's the deal
After sitting three A's. I'm delighted –
Creative subjects… short-sighted?
Not a bit of it… he's testing his talents on me.
I'm his first freelance client, you see.
I tried my poems on him:
Men In My Kitchen can go viral –
Enthusiasm I couldn't dim
You'll need a website too!
Logo was the brief…
Now, so much to do,
My favourite recipes next… good grief,
This thing's got legs!
Young minds and technology achieve
Results I couldn't believe –
When collaboration is the word
Nothing seems absurd.
Old minds think young
This thing has just begun…
Sit down and eat, grandson…

GET IN SHOT, SWEETIE! ↓ ↓ ↓ 📷 ↓ ↓ ↓ STRIKE A POSE!

#FABSQUAD

RECIPE: CHICKEN, CHEESE AND CRISP SURPRISE

This recipe evolved in a last-minute hurry to feed six hungry schoolboys who arrived... shall we say unexpectedly? On every level it was a surprise. Quick, easy and delicious, it will make you very popular. I would not (and did not) hesitate to serve it to adults and add it to my list of accidentally discovered and most enjoyable main dishes. It's ideal for large or small numbers and great for a buffet / serve-yourself sort of meal.

Ingredients:

- 4 large skinless chicken breasts
- 1-2 tins of Campbell's condensed chicken soup
- 350 grams of strong Cheddar cheese
- 1 large or 2 small packet of plain crisps

Serves 6

Method:

You will need a generous-sized oven-proof pie or Pyrex dish.

Put the oven on and warm to 180°C.

Cut the chicken breasts into bite-size chunks and place at the bottom of the dish.

Open the cans of condensed soup and spoon over. Make sure enough of the thick sauce-like contents cover the diced chicken

Grate the cheese and completely cover the surface.

Crush the crisps in the bag and sprinkle them over the cheese.

Bake for 20-25 minutes or until the top is golden and crispy.

Serve with steamed Basmati rice or a large jacket potato per person.

Garnish with herbs (of course!).

Aga
In My Kitchen

Thames View House, Summer of 1997.
A tribute to Harm, the man in my kitchen then

A Georgian gem is Thames View House
It does not disappoint. On Chiswick Mall
It proudly stands, four stories slim and tall,
And not the mightiest house of all –
Dwarfed by others snuggled close
Not vying for attention…
Yet deserving of a mention…
Neighbours' with their six-foot walls
And iron gates to deter –
I know which one I prefer.

No prying eyes and envious sighs,
It enjoys its subtle modesty,
Terraced on both sides
With little or no pomposity.
It has integrity…
It has some secrets too
I might just share with you…
Because I lived there once…
The front door was quite accessible
To knock and enter entirely possible
It had a friendly welcoming face,
Nothing forbidding here,
A cosy and thoroughly likeable place…

One thing these period houses share
Looking o'er the Thames
Is the extraordinary view
Not to be compared…
But only for the privileged few…
Oddly, separated by the street
That often disappeared
Underwater,
High spring tides were feared…
You simply could not get by
Without, at the least, very wet feet.

A dining room quietly looked out
Over a long flower filled garden.
A wonderful kitchen – hear me shout!
It had an Aga, oh great delight,
Shiny, bronze and black, what a happy sight.
This really was a dream come true…
From that time we shared together
What treats I cooked for you
Once I learned its tricky ways –
Reading instructions always pays –
The nicest thing to lean against
It's always warm so no complaints.
Many a memory of lingering meals
With music you shared, new to my ears.

With four floors and winding stairs
A drawing room with comfortable chairs
Tall French windows looking out
From which to hear oarsmen shout
As they practise at a pace
For the Oxford and Cambridge Boat Race.

That isn't all...
It had two secrets we tried to keep
But in summer out they'd seep...

A hidden front garden behind a hedge
Right beside the water's edge
It even had a weeping willow...
In the height of summer with head on a pillow
It's a dreamy place to be
So much on the water to see...

Another story I'll unfold
That is seldom ever told
Unless you come to dine...
We won't offer you wine...
Because, hidden from view
A back garden gate leads
To Fuller's Brewery... it's true!
We have beer – on tap
Now fancy that!
Absolute heaven
And often it was exactly
The perfect thing to do...
That summer of '97.
A shame it didn't last...
And went past so fast...

A new family lives there now it seems,
I stopped to say hello.
I wondered, did they too have dreams?
Come in they said and see what's been achieved.
The changes… you would not have believed.
The façade exactly the same, but the rear completely changed.
A basement and extension so beautifully arranged.
The focus on the kitchen still, which felt so strange
It stilled my heart… there
Was the same Aga, taking centre stage…
But on a different page.
Long since turned…
Much to my relief the garden was the same
As was the path leading to that gate …
And Fuller's Brewery chimney towered
Just as before…that's fate …
Covered in ivy and dense foliage used no more!
Our secret memory remains unshared… I'm glad
Not sad…
I am relieved…
Who'd have believed
They don't like beer!
And I just happened to be cycling past…
A satisfactory end …. at last.

GOOD FOOD ON THE AGA

BY
Ambrose Heath

FABER & FABER LTD.

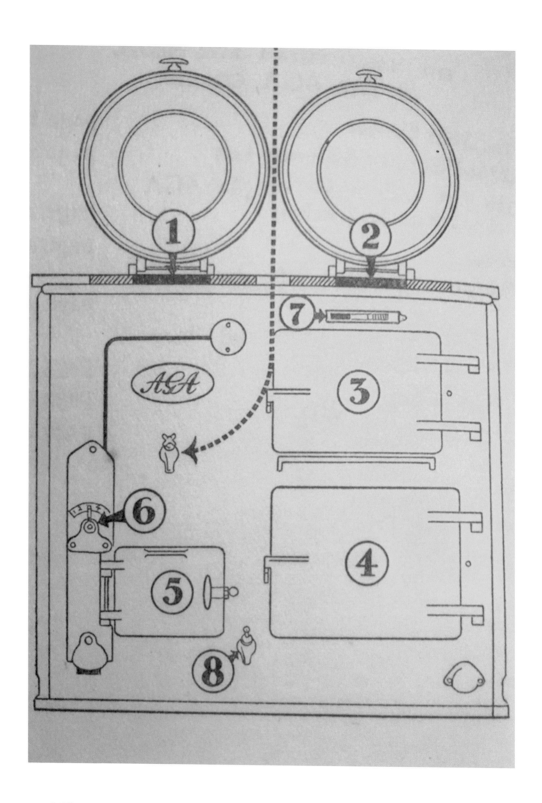

1. THE AGA COOKER

In writing of the AGA Cooker in the pages which immediately follow, it will be necessary to refer to its various parts. The explanatory diagram on the opposite page will be of help here. The different parts will be described separately in later pages.

1. This will be referred to as the left-hand hot-plate. It is the hotter of the two cooking surfaces, being used for frying, toasting, grilling and bringing liquids to the boil.

2. The right-hand, or simmering, plate.

3. The fast oven.

4. The slow oven.

5. The ash-pit door.

7. Heat indicator. This must not be regarded as an ordinary thermometer, but only as a gauge for the early morning temperature. The normal reading should be as follows:

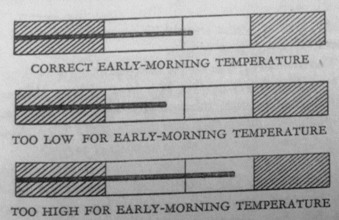

CORRECT EARLY-MORNING TEMPERATURE

TOO LOW FOR EARLY-MORNING TEMPERATURE

TOO HIGH FOR EARLY-MORNING TEMPERATURE

If, first thing in the morning, the mercury is below or above the line in the middle of the white space, the thermostat probably wants adjusting. It does not indicate any danger, but simply means that the

15

JANUARY

Crêpes Suzette

Pancake batter
Cream
Oranges
Curaçao
Brandy

Chicken pancakes have, of course, reminded us of another culinary triumph, of which King Edward VII is reputed to have been so fond—*Crêpes Suzette*.

Make a pancake batter to which you have added a liqueur-glassful of curaçao. Set aside for three hours, and just before using add a little cream. Make four pancakes and keep them warm. Now melt in a chafing-dish if possible (for this last operation ought to be done at the table itself) a piece of butter, some sugar and a good squeeze of orange or tangerine juice. When this is melted, put the pancakes in one by one, turn them over once, fold them into four so that they will all lie in the dish, throw over them a liqueur-glassful of brandy and curaçao mixed, set it alight and serve these ambrosial pancakes when the flame dies down.

AGA RECIPE BOOK

A confession: There wasn't so much cooking going on in 1997, but oh such good intentions. With a full-time new man and a demanding City business to run then, I could only dream.

I discovered the most wonderful book and read it cover to cover, never having time to put it into practise, until now.

It is a pleasure to share that dream and this book, which is as great a gift as I can give.

Good Food on the Aga by Ambrose Heath....and still in print/and online.

If you own an AGA! These recipes are sublime!

Also pretty good if you don't.

A Tennis Player In My Kitchen

Anyone for tennis?

I met him on the tennis court
At a match that got quite fraught –
He moved so well with great technique
And an eye-popping physique…
We were playing doubles –
The moment I saw those moves
I knew I was in trouble…

His tactics were quite mean
His backhand the best I'd seen
A quite irrational desire seeped in
As he pushed me around the court
Testing all the skills I had –
It was tense, it was fun,
This match had to be won…

I tried my best to impress.
My partner had to lift his game
I said as we changed ends…
No stress…
I knew he felt the same.
We did it!
Game set and match… their round
Over gin & tonic at the bar.

From the opposition no sound…
Could he hear my heart pound?
He looked at me, his eyebrows raised…
I waited for his praise…
It didn't come.
No rush for me, a magic moment to savour
The silence… such odd behaviour
It quite unsettled me
In the end… he won, dinner next,
A week went past, my place
My round….
A mood profound
I took his coat,
Still no sound…
As he quietly looked around
With that openly curious gaze
I waited for his praise,
Again…
This man is driving me insane!

The aroma of my cooking…
Pervades
That should make him mine!
He's still looking
And takes the glass I offer him
Of rosé sparkling wine…
With smoked salmon canapés
"Divine" he says,
I smile.

I had to concentrate…
Time to warm the plates
I turn my back and stir
The orange sauce so rich…
A dash of Armagnac is good
I'd already opened the red wine
To let it breathe… I hardly could.
The main course can wait…
I turn.

From this point on I must divert,
Practised though I was to flirt,
My recollection's rather vague…
And perhaps not for this page.
Suffice to say my life back then
Was a little more complicated,
Was at a different stage,
But warm memories still linger on
Leaving just a taste
Of something not quite over yet.
Now life's at a different pace…
No haste.
Precious moments don't waste…
They just improve, like wine.
Nothing to lose,
From the ordinary to the extraordinary –
Those warm memories are still mine….

RECIPE: SMOKED SALMON AND CAVIAR BLINIS

If romance is higher on your agenda than cooking the blinis from scratch... then look for "Cocktail Blinis" in your favourite food-halls or supermarkets, nestling closely to the fresh and smoked fish section. (Ready to eat, hot or cold, but nicer freshened up in the oven for 4 mins!)... He won't know and you'd be disappointed if there wasn't a little shortcut!

Ingredients:

- ¼ cup buckwheat flour
- 1 cup plain flour
- ½ teaspoon baking powder
- 200ml milk
- 1 egg
- 2 tablespoons melted butter
- 250ml cream cheese
- 2 tablespoons finely chopped chives
- Salt and freshly ground black pepper
- 250gr sliced smoked salmon
- 3 tablespoons black caviar (or a jar of lumpfish caviar, much cheaper and looks similar)
- Fresh dill and lemon wedges to garnish

Method:

Combine both flours, baking powder and salt in a bowl.

In a separate bowl whisk the milk, egg and butter, and then beat into the flour mixture.

Heat a nonstick pan over medium heat and fry a tablespoon of batter per blini for about two minutes until bubbles form on the top of the blini. Flip and cook for a further minute or until golden brown. Repeat with the remaining batter. Set aside.

Mash together the cream cheese and chives and season with salt and pepper.

Cut the salmon to fit the blinis. Add a little lemon juice and freshly grated black pepper.

To serve, top each blini with smoked salmon, then with some of the cream cheese and chive mixture. Finish with a small dollop of caviar (or lumpfish caviar) and a sprig of dill and serve with lemon wedges.

A Tailor In My Kitchen

Watch how he touches his samples of Tweeds.
Each one a story of Highland or Heath,
Of nature and nurture to satisfy need.
Of softness and colour... lovingly bequeathed
By crafters with dyes made from heather,
In whatever the weather...
They survive.
"Stop"- I draw breath,
Wide-eyed and seeing what he sees
How can I choose, from these hues, these textures?
These hardships
That will weave
Warmth into my bones.
From courage hard won
He smiles and watches
And knowingly waits.
I sigh ....

That glass table again comes into play
As he lovingly sets out his dazzling display
Of silk linings and wool soft to the touch.
I feel the love of his craft, so much
And the mystery,
The woven hardship with history
And the sheer artistry
Of patterns and symmetry.
These little samples tell it all
And mirror in his eyes.
And what of him?
Don't go there they plead.

I see the shared complexity
The love of nature
And need for nurture
Not so different from
The woven beauty of tweed   .
He gives little away.
Perplexed, vexed
Pain and passion
Never out of fashion
Tightly buttoned.
He must keep it in.
Not easily done
Emotions run deep that's clear.

Hiding behind his eloquence,
And a little false bravado
Humour hiding fear,
He has no need.
Funny and kind
A really good mind.
He's only human...
To ask himself ...
"What happened to all those years?"

I learn… of friends gone, at a cost
There's sadness…. there's pride
The sands of time march on mercilessly
Things are lost and seldom found
Life's illusions so profound
Evaporate without a sound
Yet to win what he seeks
Someone to share and care….
It's more….
forsaking himself is hard
That's clear
And has lost him much.

Will he choose nurture and comfort?
From the vastness and fabric of his trade…
The price paid.
In life, we reap what we sow (sew!)
That is how we grow and grow
Bringing that softness and colour
To his jackets of Tweed.

RECIPE: CRANACHAN

This traditional Scottish dessert is much loved and delicious – popular and a very real rival for English trifle… and so much quicker and easier!

The only cooking involved is toasting or browning the porridge oats.

Ingredients:

- 570ml (1 pint) of double cream
- 85g (3oz) of jumbo porridge oats
- 7 tbsp whisky
- 3 tbsp honey
- 450g (1lb) of fresh raspberries
- Sprig of fresh mint to garnish

Method:

Toast the oats in a frying pan, careful not to burn them.

Lightly whip the cream until it folds into peaks, then mix in the whisky and honey. Very gently, fold in the oatmeal and raspberries.

Serve in individual dessert dishes, saving a few toasted oats, raspberries and mint to garnish.

Suppliers

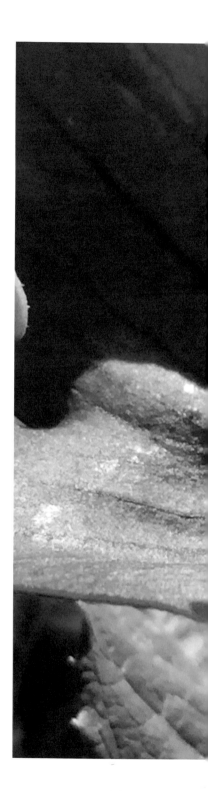

My bread recipe in "My Kitchen Knows Me Well" uses a Lakeland bread mix. Their large selection includes gluten free options, healthy, multigrain, sourdough etc. A wonderful base for adding your own choice of herbs, nuts, fruit or whatever suits the mood.
Website: **www.lakeland.co.uk**

My Doro Wat recipe for "Poet In My Kitchen" uses a great Berber spice mix made by Steenbergs Organic.
Website: **http://www.steenbergs.co.uk**

In the section "Aga In My Kitchen", I have recommended a long ago published book by Ambrose Heath, entitled "Good Food on the Aga", which is still in print and available from Persephone Books.
Website: **persephonebooks.co.uk**

I would like to thank:

LEMN SISSAY

I am so proud to be able to thank Lemn Sissay for his encouragement and support. Above all else he is a great poet, writer, broadcaster and benefactor who gives his all. And he unstintingly shares his gift for words… a kind and generous man, as Manchester University discovered when he was appointed Chancellor in 2015.

Thank you, Lemn, for inviting me to my first ever Literary Festival in March 2015, in Dubai of all places! Another new experience, which has inspired me to get out there and do something instead of just talking or thinking about it. Being surrounded by writers, poets and artists who communicate in so many wonderful ways, both personal and touching, has changed my life.

Thank you Lemn for being a great friend and an encouraging supporter of my project, *Men In My Kitchen*…

KARINNA DAMO

My friend Karinna Damo who, while I was in Florida for Thanksgiving in 2015, said as she skimmed through the photos on my iPad "There are a lot of men in your kitchen". She was right... and what a provocative sound bite.

Later that week, the poems began to flow. *Men In My Kitchen* was born.

ROBERT DEMPSTER

Robert Dempster, the Detroit writer, musician and creator of videos, whom I met by chance the following day on a sunset cruise… We shared stories and had dinner together and discovered a shared passion for photography. He liked my first poem and suggested that I write more… and I have.

CAPTIVA ISLAND

ROGER EATON

And Roger Eaton, my cinematographer friend, who also shares my passion for film and photography. Ever since we met at a film premier we have collaborated in the script writing and production of his own work and he is helping with sound, video recording and additional photos for *Men In My Kitchen*.

OSCAR LINES

Oscar's story is yet to be written. His life and decisions are ahead of him. You will have a flavour of what might be to come from the poem about him in this series and from our logo…
Thank you Oscar, for your creativity and collaboration with our designer for the Linda Lines logo, fitting so well to become one with *Men In My Kitchen*… Very nicely done!
Your very first freelance commission…
May there be many more…

To find out more about Linda Lines and her writing projects, and to keep up with her latest news visit her website: lindalines.co.uk

If you have enjoyed this book, please leave a review on Amazon. Linda would love to know what you thought.

Girls In The City... on its way for 2018.

Girls in the City is the flip side of *Men In My Kitchen*.

This will be my second book and also contains a series of poems based on true stories, illustrated with dramatic photos of the City of London and supported not by recipes but by favourite watering holes – pubs, clubs and wine bars – established and new, where the true business of the City is conducted. Popular drinks, like fashion, change with the times. A little history of those favourite places and tipples, from wines, spirits, beers and ciders to cocktails, will be given with photos and recipes.

NOTES

NOTES

Lightning Source UK Ltd.
Milton Keynes UK
UKRC02n0132271017
311713UK00007B/30